In a Quiet Village

by Leonisa S. Merced-Malana

RoseDog❖Books

PITTSBURGH, PENNSYLVANIA 15222

All Rights Reserved
Copyright 2003 Leonisa S. Merced-Malana
No part of this book may be reproduced or transmitted
in any form or by any means, electronic or mechanical,
including photocopying, recording, or by any information
storage and retrieval system without permission in
writing from the author.

ISBN # 0-8059-9260-X
Printed in the United States of America

First Printing

For information or to order additional books, please write:
RoseDog Books
701 Smithfield St.
Third Floor
Pittsburgh, PA 15222
U.S.A.
1-866-834-1803
Or visit our web site and on-line bookstore at www.rosedog.com

Dedication

This book is dedicated to my parents, Patricio and Magdalena Merced, on their 65th Wedding Anniversary;

To my brothers and sisters: Antonio, Mercedes, Virgilio, Rolando, Renato, Cynthia, Cesar and Oscar, Amancio and Rodrigo;

To my children: Dione, Romeo, Lenissa, Florante Jr., and Magnolia;

And especially to the good people of my hometown: Aritao, Nueva Vizcaya.

Acknowledgement

I want to thank my brother,
Virgilio Merced for his support, assistance and encouragement in the completion of this journal.

My Parents
Patricio and Magdalena Merced

Aritao, My Hometown

The year was 1937. I was one year old when my parents migrated to this little town called Aritao, Nueva Vizcaya, in the northern part of the Philippines. My father, Patricio M. Merced was the telegraph operator in Baliuag, Bulacan where he met my mother, Magdalena Santos, and eventually married her in 1935. I called my father "*Tatang*" and my mother "*Inang*". I was christened Leonisa Vicenta but my folks called me Nisa for short. I am their firstborn.

Tatang was born in Santa Cruz, Zambales where he spent his childhood. They were mostly farmers. My grandfather, Felipe (*Lolo Peping*) was also a "*hilot*" or quack doctor. He was quite well known in the area, as he was responsible for delivering most of the babies in Santa Cruz, and in the neighboring towns and barrios. He was also known as a *herbolario* who was able to cure diseases using herbs and grains. Apparently, Tatang was not satisfied with the lifestyle in Santa Cruz, so when he reached high school, he left with his carabao and traveled on foot to Muñoz, Nueva Ecija. The trip took almost a week and he related to us that he would spend the nights on the road where he would tie the leash of his carabao to his feet while he slept so it would not be stolen. Midway, in Lingayen, Pangasinan, he sold the carabao and caught the bus to Muñoz where he enrolled at the Central Luzon Agricultural School. He eventually finished High School and later was trained as a radio operator.

Leonisa S. Merced-Malana

Inang was born and raised in Baliuag, Bulacan. She only knew her mother, Rosario Santos, a half sister Marita, a half brother, Raul and her stepfather Angel. As a child, she helped with the family income by selling strings in the *sabungan*. According to her, she met a man who became very friendly with her. He would buy all the strings she had for sale. That went on everyday that she was there so she became suspicious and felt very uncomfortable every time she saw him. She later found out that he was her father, Francisco De Leon from Hagunoy, Bulacan and that she was his illegitimate child. She also learned that she had another half sister by him, Salvacion.

I suppose the best thing that ever happened to me was to grow up in this beautiful town of Aritao with its friendly people living simple lives. Although I was born in Baliuag, I could not imagine myself living in that busy town, very industrialized, in the outskirts of Manila. The weather was always hot, the air dusty with all the noise from the different businesses around.

Reaching Aritao took almost ten hours by bus going north from Manila on dusty gravel roads passing thru the flat agricultural lands of the Central Plains of Luzon until it reaches the town of San Jose, Nueva Ecija. Continuing north on San Jose, the road leaves the Central Plains of Luzon and enters the Caraballo mountain range where it begins the ascent along steep mountain cliffs and narrow gravel roads that occasionally gave way to landslides during the rainy season. Going up the mountains ended at Balete Pass, the highest point in the national highway.

This place is known historically as the place where General Yamashita offered the strongest resistance when the Allied Forces came to liberate the Philippines from the Japanese Military Forces. In the battle of May 31, 1945, 7064 Japanese soldiers were killed and 2000 soldiers of the US army 25th division were either killed or wounded [i]. Balete Pass is also known as Dalton Pass in honor of General James Dalton of the 25th division who was killed there.

Dalton Pass divides the provinces of Nueva Vizcaya to the north and Nueva Ecija to the south. After reaching the peak where a monument was built to commemorate the fall of Balete Pass, the road then begins its descent over sharp curves and pigtail highways.

In A Quiet Village

From up the mountain peak, you could see the tiny town of Santa Fe and as you continued zigzagging down, the town became bigger until you finally reached it after a sharp and steep curve. As you stepped out of the bus for a short rest, you could feel the change in the climate; the temperature got cooler and the air, fresher. Santa Fe was only about a half mile long and the only street was lined with restaurants and stores selling handicrafts of Igorot products. The next town is Aritao, which would become my hometown.

Aritao, founded in 1665 is a picturesque small town nestled between the mountain ranges of the Caraballo and the Cordillera[ii]. On the distant east is the mountain range of the Sierra Madre. From the south, it is the second town in the province of Nueva Vizcaya, the gateway to the Cagayan Valley in northern Philippines. The name ARITAO was coined after the words from the Isinay dialect, *ARI,* [King] and *TAU,* [our], meaning Our King. The king referred to was a brave warrior, Ari Mengal, an Igorot chief who defied Spanish missionaries. He lived in an early settlement originally called Ajanas, which in Igorot term meant a place of abundance. Ajanas was then changed to Aritao in honor of this king[iii].

Aritao was bordered on the north by the Igorot town of Kayapa, on the northeast by Bambang, on the east by Dupax and the south by Santa Fe and the boundary lines of the province of Nueva Ecija.

The national highway spanned approximately one and a half kilometers from the southwest to the northeast end of the town proper. The continuation of the Santa Fe River flowed alongside the highway on the east. There were endless mountains all over; we coined the names of these mountains according to our fancy. All the mountains surrounding the town were bald. One of them was Mount Malusong or to us kids was *Bantay Lakay*, [old man]. This mountain was bald all over except for a few trees at its peak and it resembled an old man sitting and watching the town nestled at its feet. Across the river was *Comon Rock*, standing guard as you entered the barrio of Comon and Gasahas and was observed by picnickers to have big boulders of rocks scattered all over. At the southern part of the town and easily seen from the river is Mount Orden or *Kuplat* known for it's flat peak [flat top].

My parents rented a small house from Mr. and Mrs. Eleazar

Author at 4 years old

In A Quiet Village

Caoile in the center of the town. We were a couple of blocks from the centuries old Catholic Church, built between 1777 and 1786 [iv]. The church was built facing the municipal building, typical of Spanish colonial towns. There, Tatang worked at the Post Office. He was the Postmaster-Operator. Our place was also near the public market, on the backside of town.

I never remembered having a clock at home. We kept time by the tolling of the church bells that announced six o'clock in the morning, twelve o'clock noon, and six o'clock in the evening, times meant for us to pray the "Angelus". The church bells spoke to us. I knew when there were happy occasions or sad ones by the ringing of the bells. Of course, there was the routine sound announcing the daily morning mass. The first ring was slow and monotonous, then after a few minutes, the second ring became very fast, like saying, "*Hurry up! The mass is about to start*". On Sundays and Holidays, the small bells rang on a joyous mood after each mass, in the same manner that celebrations such as baptisms and weddings were proclaimed to the entire town. During a funeral, the slow, moaning sounds of the big, bass bells told you to "*hush up, pray for someone who has passed away*", as the funeral cortege entered and left the church. And on Easter Sundays, all the bells would peal in unison as if singing the "*Gloria In Excelsis Deo*". On this special occasion, pulling on the bell ropes would not suffice. The *sacristans* would climb up the belfry and turn the bells on their fulcrum nonstop, until they reached the point of exhaustion. As the bells ring on Easter Sunday, the kids were supposed to jump up and down, wherever they may be, to enhance their growth.

Being new in town, Inang was scared and uneasy, not knowing the culture and customs of the townspeople. One morning, she heard someone pumping water from the well located in front of the house. When she peeked out the window, she saw a man with only a G-string around his waist. Scared, she hurriedly took me in her arms and ran to the Post Office where my father was. She finally learned that this guy was an Igorot and that was how they dressed up.

The population consisted of the native *Isinays* and the immigrants of *Ilocanos, Tagalogs, Pangasinensis, Kapampangans* and a few Chinese. All of these groups have their own dialect but then, the *Ilocano* and the *Tagalog* became the most commonly used. I could say that we were well versed in these two dialects and since some of my friends spoke *Isinay*, we were also fluent in this.

The majority of the people were Roman Catholics. The other religions were Protestants, *Sabadistas*, [Seventh Day Adventists], *Saksi Ni Jeovah*, [Jehovah's Witness], some *Aglipays* and *Iglesia Ni Cristo*. The religions of *Aglipay* and *Iglesia Ni Cristo* originated in the Philippines. Augustinian, Belgian and Dominican priests took turns in running the predominant Catholic Church. Franciscan nuns were also assigned there.

Superstition and folklore, unique customs and mores played important roles in peoples' lives. After somebody died, the soul of the departed was offered food first, before each meal. This was called "*atang*". The food was placed on the altar or thrown outside the house while saying, "*kayu-kayu*", calling to the spirit of the dead. On the third, ninth and fortieth days after death, the soul of the deceased was believed to come back and may reveal his/her presence in the form of the scent of fragrant flowers or of a burning candle, the howling of dogs, or the occurrence of something unusual such as the falling and breaking of a glass or china or the plain gushing of the wind.

Mounds of earth called *buntons* were avoided because it was believed to be the dwelling place of the *kaibaan*, or evil spirits, and one should never make them angry or else, one will suffer unpleasant consequences.

When a child is exposed for the first time to a stranger, that person is supposed to lay his/her hand on the forehead of the child to prevent him/her from being *ma-am-am-lingan* or becoming vulnerable to catching a disease or bad *karma*.

The *manggagamud*, similar to a witch is most dreaded. He/she could be anybody you know or don't know and could cast a spell in the form of a dreadful disease like unexplained tumors or the presence of foreign bodies inside a person, or physical ailments that medical science can not cure or explain. This is supposed to be revenge from the manggagamud and it is only thru him/her that the ailment can be cured.

The role of a hilot was very significant. At that time, there was

In A Quiet Village

no medical doctor available. Only a Public Health Nurse and a Sanitary Inspector ran the Municipal Health Center. The hilot was believed to possess a special skill with her hands and was one of those called to deliver babies or to attend to persons who are ill using oil or other herbs as medicines. They are very popular in the cure for *pilay* [broken bones or joint pains] thru the use of massage. Like my Lolo Peping in Santa Cruz, Aling Maria [Llena] was the most known hilot in Aritao. I could remember her attending to Inang every time she gave birth to my brothers and sisters. She would come everyday for ten days to massage Inang.

The *Igorots* lived in the mountain towns of Pingkian and Kayapa. They came down regularly especially on market days to trade their goods consisting of coffee, *camote*, *guisantes*, potatoes, ginger, and handicrafts of brooms, baskets and other products made of rattan and bamboo and wood carvings. They maintained their native costumes of G-strings for the men and colorful skirts and blouses and gold bracelets for the women.

One moonless night, when it was quiet everywhere, the sudden barking of the dogs startled me. This was followed by the rolling of drums, then a piercing cry of "*Dinggen yu kailian,*" or "Hear ye, town mates... etc.". I was very scared, I ducked under the table to hide. I knew Inang was also scared as she did not understand what was going on. The next day, we learned that this was the *bandolero* delivering messages from the municipal Mayor to the people. Since there were no newspapers, the town crier went from block to block to announce new ordinances or other important events. This was their form of communication.

Growing up easily exposed us to the different habits and practices that children were up to imitate. I was always fascinated watching the old folks prepare and chew the *ma-má,* a beetle-nut concoction. This was composed of the beetle nut, the green leaf called *ga-wed* and the fine white powder known as *apog*. These were mixed together and chewed producing very bright red saliva that was then spat out. My friends and I tried to chew this *ma-má*. The taste was pungent and burning and before long our salivas turned red and we imitated the old folks in spitting it out. What we did not expect was the spinning of the head and the dizziness we

Leonisa S. Merced-Malana

experienced as an aftermath. We also tried to imitate the women smoking their cigars or cigarettes with the lighted end inside their mouths, resulting in several burns of our tongues and lips.

After a year, my brother, Anton was born. Since we did not have any relatives in town, my mother opted to deliver him in Malolos, Bulacan where her sister, Salvacion was residing and working at the Malabon General Hospital. When we came back, my grandmother, *Lola* Charing, *Tia* Marita, *Tio* Raul and their father, *Lolo* Angel came to live with us until my sister Mercy was born and the Second World War erupted after the bombing of Pearl Harbor in 1941.

The War Years

Evacuation! I could but faintly remember the first time we had to leave the comfort and familiarity of home and escape to the wilderness for safety. War had come to our peaceful Aritao. It was in 1941, right after the bombing of Pearl Harbor. I was five years old. My sister, Mercy, was four months old.

I could remember climbing a steep mountain in the middle of the night. Tatang tied a hollow bamboo tube on my back containing water to drink. According to our guide, the reason we traveled by night was because the mountain was so steep and traveling in the dark would prevent us from looking down the terrain below and that would be easier for us. Mr. Eladio Dalan, the assistant postmaster and his wife Cornelia who was the Puericulture Center nurse, came to evacuate with us.

Inang explained that the reason we were leaving town was because the Japanese invaded our country and that they were looking specifically for Tatang because he was the telegraph operator. It was not clear to me whether they wanted him for his services or because he was considered an enemy.

Soon we reached a place with a waterfall, huge stones and a shallow brook. This was called Noknok. My father decided to camp there. He built us a hut made of felled trees, cogon roof and palm leaves as walls. The trees were so tall you could hardly see the sky and the sun's rays that rarely filtered through.

Leonisa S. Merced-Malana

Below the waterfall was a brook, with crystal clear water. Scattered all over the area were granite stones of different sizes; some were so huge that we were not able to climb them. We went to the brook to bathe every morning. We used a shampoo called *gugo* that was extracted from the bark of a tree. We also did our laundry using the same gugo for soap.

One night, the monsoon rains came, followed by the swarming of very tiny insects called *sipsip*. Before long, I was scratching all over, my body covered with insect bites. Inang kept me inside a mosquito net all day until the itch subsided.

Inang said we stayed in Noknok for a few weeks. We then went down to the barrio of Tabueng located near the foot of the mountain. We stayed with the Canuto Duque family until it was certain that it was safe to go back to town. Tatang resumed his duties as Postmaster-Telegraph operator. The Japanese have occupied my hometown, Aritao.

When I first saw the Japanese soldiers, I thought they came from another world. They looked very scary with their fatigue uniforms and funny looking hats with flaps behind the ears. Their shoes were also different in that the big toe was separated from the rest. I was in grade one or grade two and was introduced to the Japanese language that was incorporated in the curriculum. We were instructed on their alphabet, the *Katakana*, as well as to their arithmetic and learned how to sing the Japanese national anthem, *Kimi Gayo*, and other Japanese songs. They also taught the women how to cook *mochi*, a Japanese delicacy made of steamed sweet rice.

During the Japanese occupation, I heard a lot of atrocities done by the Japanese, especially the killing of Filipino soldiers in the public market and the torture of some relatives of Filipino soldiers or those suspected of helping the guerillas. But the Japanese I knew were different. Maybe, this was so because they were not combat soldiers.

There was a Japanese doctor, his name I could not recall, who was a very good physician and was responsible for tending to the sick in the community. Sometimes, he came to the house, carried me on his shoulders and played with me. He showed me pictures of his family back in Japan and I thought he was a rather lonesome

In A Quiet Village

man, away from his home. He sometimes took me and my friends, Nelda and Charing to eat out. He made us some Japanese kimonos and taught us how to sing and dance to the tune of a Japanese song, *Sikararete*.

There were also other Japanese who were in charge of the rice granaries and food supplies. They would occasionally give us some canned goods and yards of clothing materials, some are made of abaca and called *pinukpok*.

The garrison compound was located across the municipal building and was guarded by sentries twenty-four hours a day. Everyone who passed through had to stop and bow to the guards. At first, this ritual fascinated me. My friends and I would purposely pass by the guardhouse several times just to demonstrate our well-practiced bows, at times accompanied by uncontrolled giggles. There was one Japanese guard that we really loved to tease. We called him Maswi San. It was not long before the guards noticed our pranks and started shooing us off with their *Kura! Kura!*

After we became more settled, Inang started the Bulakeña restaurant where my Lolo Angel became the chief cook. He was really good at his trade and the restaurant became popular, especially with the *viajeros* and *pasaheros*. Many days after coming home hungry, I would just go to the counter and chose whatever I wanted from the row of specially prepared food on display. This was a real treat considering what we went through during the evacuation.

The second evacuation was more vivid in my mind. The year was 1944. I was sitting in our balcony pulling a string attached to a *duyan* where my baby brother Biyong was sleeping. He was only a few months old. Suddenly and out of nowhere, I heard a loud eerie sound that I could not figure out, as this was the first time I heard it. Then I saw two dark objects that looked like giant bees in the sky, which I later learned were airplanes. Confused and frightened I ran aimlessly, and when I saw my Tio Raul run towards the river, I followed him. I saw Inang running too. For some reason, she kept going back and forth toward the house as if she had forgotten something. Then she realized that instead of my brother Biyong, who was still sleeping soundly in the hammock, she grabbed a pillow in her frantic effort to get out of the house. She went back and with my brother in her arms, we trekked towards the river. I remembered diving into the water every time the big planes swooped down, thinking that the water will protect me from whatever catastrophe that was on hand.

After the planes left, we went back to the house to wait for my father who was at work. We later learned that those were American planes. They were coming to liberate us from the Japanese. Once again, we had to make plans to evacuate the town to escape the perils of armed engagements.

This time, we did not go very far. We settled in the small barrio of Kasay, short of a mile across the river. The nuns from the convent came to stay with us for there was nobody else to help them. The Hidalgo sisters also evacuated with us. One of the sisters, we call her Auntie Pacing, just lost her husband. My father, my uncle and my Lolo were the only males in our group and they were the ones who built the temporary shelters where we stayed.

Tatang dug a huge tunnel adjacent to our hut. It was large enough to accommodate several sacks of rice and other staples such as canned goods, sugar and salt. We also slept there at night and took cover when the bombings became rampant.

Every day, after the bombings, Tatang and I went to town to scavenge anything that we could use. Sometimes, we were able to get some burned salt, rice, or canned goods. There were times when I carried two or three pieces of galvanized iron or pieces of wood on my head. These were used to fortify our huts for roofing and posts. Tatang would boil the burned salt until it dried giving us ample supply of crystal white salt, a very rare commodity on those days.

The trips to town after the air raids were scary. One day, at the *sasalugan*, we passed by the body of a soldier probably dead for several days. His body was black and bloated, and swarms of flies covered it. The stench was indescribable and it took several days before I got used to the situation and learned to ignore the unpleasant conditions.

As days went by, we learned to make use of the food from the land. Since there was no husked rice available, we pounded the rice

In A Quiet Village

from the harvested stalks. First we gathered fresh carabao manure, put it in a pail and mixed it with our feet until it formed a pasty consistency. Then we spread the paste evenly on the ground, covering a wide enough area. After the manure dried, it formed a cement-like covering over the dusty ground. The whole procedure was called *galem*.

Using an *al-o'*, we pounded the palay on the cemented ground to separate the grain from the stalk. Then the palay grain was transferred to an *alsong*, and the pounding continued until all the husks were stripped, exposing the white grain. The alsong is carved from the trunk of a tree with a hollow space in the center to contain the palay to be pounded. One, two or three persons can pound using the al-o, also carved from a piece of wood. The cadence of the pounding follows the rhythm of one, one-two, or one-two-three, according to the number of persons participating in the exercise. After the husks are gone, the white grains are transferred to a wide and flat bamboo basket called *biga-o*. The procedure called winnowing follows by tossing the grains to the air so that the wind will blow away dust residues leaving the rice grains clean and ready for cooking.

For other foods we dug (*kur-it),* tiny snails embedded in the dry rice paddies and gathered *kangkong* leaves from the pond. Sometimes we would gather *kalunay* that grew around the yard and the rice fields. Roasted palay grains substituted for coffee.

As the bombings continued, we noticed more and more Japanese coming and going. Some of them built huts near our place and I thought they also came there to hide. Every day, Inang went by their doorstep and hid their shoes before the airplanes came.

We were able to predict when the air raids occurred. Usually there was a lone plane with a monotonous drone; we called it the *tutubi* [dragonfly]. We figured this was an observation plane, for after a few minutes; the bomber planes came fast, usually in pairs and released the bombs. As soon as the planes came, we would dash to the tunnel for safety. As days passed by, we were sure that we were not the targets of the bombings. Some of us stayed outside to watch as the raids went on.

I was awakened at dawn one morning when I felt a heavy, cold thing on my chest. I could hardly breath because of its weight. I screamed and when Inang came, she saw me covered from my chest to my toes with earth that fell from the side of the tunnel. My cousin, Erlinda, who was just a couple of days old, and also my brother, Anton were also buried. That same morning, we found out that one of the cannons released that night hit the hut of the nuns nearby and the Mother Superior, Mother Imelda was killed.

The day I can never forget was the day the "*makapili*" came to the house. The *makapilis* were the most dreaded persons during that time. They were considered as spies for the Japanese or traitors and no one really knew which side they were on. They were strangers in our community coming from the neighboring provinces.

The makapili came early that morning. He spent some time talking with Tatang. We were still in the foxhole and my brothers and sister were still asleep. Tatang looked very sad and worried when he showed up at the entrance of the hole.

Inang told us that according to the guy, Tatang would be picked up at 3:00 PM that afternoon and would be shot. Inang did not tell us the reason why. We did not know what to do. I was horrified, knowing that something like this could truly happen. There were already a few of our friends or relatives who were either killed or have disappeared. One of them was my Tio Peling, Tia Marita's husband and the father of my cousin Erlinda. He disappeared one day and never came back.

Inang had to do something. She sought advise from our neighbors and one of them was Mrs. Patricia Sayo, a well-known and respected lady and the owner of Botica Sayo. She suggested offering the makapil*i* some money in exchange for the freedom of Tatang. I knew Inang went out seeking help from our friends to raise some money for she did not come home right away. For us, the agony of waiting was almost unbearable. I was praying and wishing to stop or slow down the clock to delay the time. Three o'clock came but the makapili did not show up. Whatever happened after that, we never knew. The man did not come back to carry his threat. Probably, he himself was on the run because that same week, we learned that he had been shot to death. Nevertheless, the horrible memory of that day would continue to haunt me for years.

In A Quiet Village

A few days later, we were going to be liberated by the Allied Forces. I believe it was the first week of June, 1945. From our evacuation place across the river, we could see the national road in barrio Cutar where the caravan of soldiers filled the highway as they advanced towards the town. People were jubilant but were subdued, as there were still some Japanese soldiers around.

I was sitting by the door of our hut when a Japanese soldier came. He looked very thin and was hungry. He came asking for some food. When our neighbors saw him, they grabbed a piece of wood and started hitting him on the head until he fell and died in front of me. I was both terrified and angry with the people; however, I could not do anything. The people had so much anger for the Japanese soldiers but had not been able to fight back. Now that the allied soldiers were advancing, they felt that this was the time for revenge. The soldier was buried in front of our hut with his feet sticking out.

The same day the allied soldiers came, we prepared to go back to town. We built a temporary hut at the lot owned by the Catholic Church. Here, we would stay until we found a more permanent place.

The allied soldiers were a contrast to the Japanese in general. They were very friendly and gave us children a lot of candies, chewing gum, chocolate and cigarettes for the men. Sometimes, we children would fall in line after the last soldier for some food during mealtime as they gave out the rations. This was the first time that we tasted chili con carne and vegetable soup western style. In the evenings some of them will come to the house for a friendly chat.

Even after the liberation, we were not spared in witnessing more violence, this time from my town mates. Every day, a convoy of trucks passed by carrying loads of Japanese prisoners. As the trucks approached the town, people threw stones at the captured soldiers injuring many. The American soldiers could not do anything except to drive past the town in a hurry. Later, they made sure that the trucks were covered with canvas to protect the prisoners.

After a few months, my parents were able to buy a lot not too far from where we were staying and across the municipal building.

Leonisa S. Merced-Malana

The house we built was made of *sawali* walls and bamboo floors. I could remember how on my free time, I would perch on the unfinished floor and watched as the carpenter, Tino Escobedo arranged and nailed each piece of wood to complete the house. In this house, my brothers Rolando (*Bing*), Renato (*Rene*) and my sister Cynthia (*Panchang*) were born, followed by the two sets of twins, Cesar (Idal) and Oscar *(Odal)*, then Amancio (*Amang*) and Rodrigo (*Ig-ig*).

Soon the bitter memories of war would slowly fade for I finally began to enjoy and savor the sweetness of my childhood as I grew up with my brothers and sisters under the loving care of Tatang and Inang.

The Growing Years

The afternoon sun was sizzling as I walked down the road on my way home. School has ended and the students were all in a hurry when the bell rang announcing the noon break.

As I approached our house, I could smell the food that Inang was cooking. My stomach growled. I was very hungry. I speeded my steps until I reached home. I was relieved to see that the table was ready for lunch. The food was fried *hito*, and a salad of boiled *kamote* tops with diced tomatoes and *bagoong*. I was about to dash for my plate but Inang gave me that disapproving look. Tatang has not arrived and so we have to wait for him.

Discipline was well observed at home. Inang taught us good behavior in a way that *"looks"* from her would suffice to let you know if your manners were acceptable or not. The inevitable lashes from her slippers were used only as a last resort, depending on the gravity of one's misbehavior. The tone of voice was also crucial because nobody was allowed to yell back when being scolded.

There was a tall *Caballero* tree beside our old house. When the rainy season starts, this tree would be full of bright red blossoms as if it was on fire. It is also believed that during this time, the courting season for the Ilongots, one of the native tribes in the region starts. This was very significant because according to tradition, for a male to be able to marry, he must present a human head to the father of the bride in order to show his bravery and worthiness. Thus, we were cautioned not to stay out after dark during this season.

Tatang attached a swing on one of the branches of the Caballero. After school, I would go to the swing and "fly" as high as I could, singing at the top of my voice my favorite songs that I learned. There I would spend the rest of the afternoon until Tatang would call me because it would be dark and the mosquitoes would soon be hovering over. That was one place I loved to be, away from everyone, just singing and daydreaming.

My parents were strict Catholics and that was how we were raised. Church activities were encouraged. I remembered the classes in Catechism I attended with Miss Elena Mañago as our teacher. She became a very close friend of the family such that we learned to call her "Auntie Elen", adopting her as a relative. She told us that she used to be a nun. She served the Church not only as a Catechist; she was also in charge of decorating the altar according to the liturgical seasons. When there was a death in the neighborhood, she would be expected to lead the prayers during the wake.

Our parish priest was Father Willy. He would allow us to play in his rectory and if we did well in the Catechism classes, he would give us a lot of *stampitas*. After our First Communion, we were supposed to go to confession every Saturday, attend mass and receive Holy Communion on Sundays and Holidays.

As I grew older, I was invited to join the church choir. I was the youngest in the group that was composed of older folks, mostly Isinays. The choir director was *Ama* Dico Laroza, with Mr. Juan Mallo, Municipal Treasurer, Maria Laroza, Aling Mallo, Arcadio Toje, *Ina Idi'*, *Manang Ida'* and others whom I could not recall as members. The organist was Mr. Melchor Abingayan but we always called him Menol. He had a folding organ, very old, which he carried on his back and was manually powered with the foot pedals. He never went to music school as far as I knew, but he could play any song that was requested of him. At any rate, whether he could read music notes or not, we were able to breeze through the Latin masses by Concone and Batman which I later memorized in their entirety.

Occasionally, I would be invited to sing on special occasions, on school programs or joining other musical groups as a guest singer.

Author with a musical group from barrio Banganan

Leonisa S. Merced-Malana

Every day, after lunch, Inang would require us to take a nap or siesta. But first, she would ask us to pull out her gray hair one by one. She would give us one penny for each gray hair pulled. Or, for us girls, she would go over our hair with a suyod, fine-toothed comb, to hunt for lice that seemed to be always there no matter how often we shampooed with kerosene. Then, she would leave us alone to sleep. After we woke up, there would be a *merienda* of boiled *camote* or *ginatan, suman* or *monay* or anything else that she could cook. In the evenings, after supper, we always prayed the Rosary. All activities for the rest of the night would wait until we finished our prayers.

As our family grew bigger, Inang tried to augment Tatang's earnings by opening a *Sari-sari* store. She sold all kinds of things including furniture, clothes, slippers and even coffins. I could remember my brothers, especially Biyong, Bing and Rene hiding in the upright coffins as they played hide and seek with their friends.

Tatang on the other hand spent his time off work by planting trees and vegetables in our backyard. We had Avocado and *kaimito* trees as well as *duhat*, banana, and s*uha*. Our tomatoes were of different varieties and the yard fence was covered with crawling *upo* and *kalabasa*.

Carlina Valdez came to stay with us when she was very young. She hailed from Gasajas, a small barrio across the river, and at the foot of Comon Rock. She was in the elementary school and practically grew up with us and was treated as part of the family. She helped in taking care of my brothers and sisters and in our daily chores. We called her Carling.

Ching, Tiyo Rauls daughter, our cousins from Santa Cruz, Zambales, Jovencia, Percy and Sabel came every now and then to stay with us.

The household would not be complete without the pets. We had a dog we named Minda who was with us for several years. She had a lot of offspring but it was her son Kibul whom I remembered best. He was a very good guard dog and would bark at all strangers passing by. Inang also had a pig called Peggy. In the afternoons, I helped in feeding her with leftovers mixed with *darak* and wild plants called *ngalog*. She loved to have her belly scratched. Every

Biyong, Mercy, Anton and Nisa (Author)
1948

Family picture with grandfather, Lolo Peping
Cousins Percy and Sabel and Carling Valdez

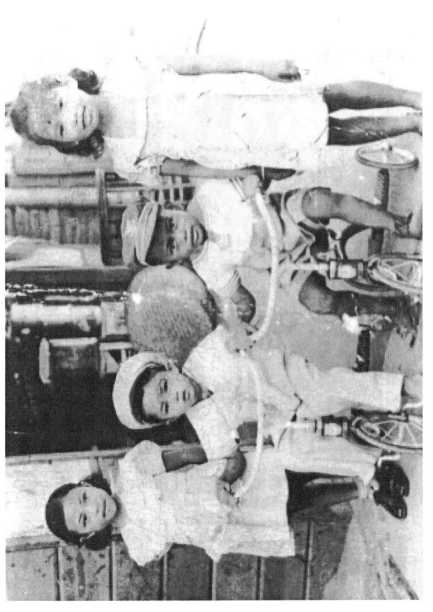

Mercy and Virgilio with friends Ciriaco (Boy) and Nellie Dulay

My eight brothers, starting from the back clockwise: Antonio, Virgilio, Rolando. Renato, Rodrigo, Amancio, Oscar, and Cesar

In A Quiet Village

six months, she would give birth to six or seven piglets. Inang would sell them so we would have enough money to pay for our tuition fees and other school expenses. Tatang also had poultry of native chicken as well as the foreign kind, the white leghorns. This gave us ample supply of chicken and eggs.

Every year, in June, Inang would prepare us for the coming school year. First, there was the dreaded "*purga*" in the form of Castor oil, a horrible tasting substance. This was supposed to clean our stomachs and intestines. We took this in the evening and before dawn, surely, our stomachs would be empty after the effect of the laxative. Then there was the visit of Mr. Genaro Galindez, the Sanitary Health Inspector with his vaccines against Cholera, Dysentery and Typhoid. Funny, because every time he came to the house, there were no children around. We either climbed the tamarind tree of our neighbor, Mr. Fermin Austria or took long walks as far from the house as possible, to escape the needles. My brother Bing and sister Cynthia would hide in the house of Auntie Elen who happened to be Cynthia's *Ninang*.

However, the best part for this time of the year was the visit to Manang Ida, the seamstress. Inang would see to it that my sisters and I had at least six new clothes and underwear, shoes and *bakya*; for my brothers, new pants, shirts and shoes before school began and of course, we should not be without the much-needed *capote* [raincoat]. For all our new clothes, Inang would require that we wear them first to church. We were growing so fast and every year, our clothes and shoes would no longer fit us.

During the rainy season, we would play with paper bankas that we made ourselves from old newspapers, and floated them in the swollen canal by the road. When the rain was accompanied by a thunderstorm, Inang would call us to stay inside the house. We were not allowed to stay near a mirror nor wear bright red clothes because the "lightning might strike us." Sometimes, the rain would stay on for several days (*nepnep*). Since we could hardly go out to play, I would just sit by the window as long as I could and watched the pitter patter of the raindrops as they hit the window panes and daydreamed or listened to it as it pounded on the roof all night.

After school, my friends would come to spend the rest of the afternoon in Inang's store. We usually shared reading the newspaper, *The Manila Daily Bulletin*, or the vernacular magazines, *Liwayway* in Tagalog and *Bannawag* in Ilocano.

At home, especially in the evenings, music played a major part in our daily activities. I could remember Inang singing *Kundimans* when she lulled my younger brothers to sleep. *Tatang's* favorite songs were "Pagan Love Song" and "Indian Love Call". My friends would come to the house with their ukelele and spend the evening strumming and singing, especially on moonlit nights. Tatang would encourage us to join in the group singing and harmonizing.

Naraniag A Bulan
(A Moonlit Night)

"*Patalunton, Patariktik*". The children were gathering on the street in front of our house, calling to all the folks, kids and grown-up alike. It was the full moon and the whole valley was enjoying its splendor. There was no electricity in town so we always took advantage of the moonlight nights to play. This night, there were no clouds in the sky as the monsoon rains ended a couple of days ago.

We have finished our supper and after putting away the dishes, everybody gathered before the small altar in the living room to pray the Rosary. I began to feel uneasy, thinking that my friends were already waiting outside. I wanted Inang to hurry, as she was leading the Rosary; in fact, I have to mumble my response of "Holy Mary, Mother of God, etc." so fast in order to finish the prayers right away. After the Rosary followed the Litany which I felt took forever. It seemed to me that the more I wanted Inang to hurry, the more petitions to all the Saints were added to our prayers. " Enough, enough," I would murmur to myself as I fidgeted in my chair.

Across the street was the sari-sari store of Mr. Ciriaco Dulay, fondly known as *Acong* in the neighborhood. What was so dear to us in *Tata Acong's* store was the loudspeaker that he put on every night, playing current music. I already heard him play "Tennessee Waltz", "Crazy", "Detour", and "Mocking Bird Hill". After a while, someone started calling my name in the loudspeaker, a reminder that the games will soon begin.

Leonisa S. Merced-Malana

I could not concentrate on the prayers. Finally, Inang said her "Amen". We took turns to kiss Tatang and Inang's hands (*mano*), as we customarily did after the evening prayers, then I fled down the flight of stairs and joined my friends waiting for me outside. Ising, Ap'ped and her older sister, Uding with her husband, Desi, were already waiting. In a while, my other friends and *kababata*, Junior, Joaquin, Romy and Timot joined us. Of course, Tata Acong's children, Carding, Romy, Nelly and Boy were also there, starting to warm up.

Desi had already fetched the water to mark the dirt road for our game of *Patalunton*. This game required two teams. One team would try to get to the other end of a rectangle that was divided into four or six squares, depending on the number of players. The other team would guard the squares and block anyone who tried to get through.

There were many players tonight. The younger kids who were not able to join the games formed their own groups and played "hide and seek" instead. The older folks sat on the benches that Tatang built around the Avocado tree in front of our house and got involved in talking about the day's news, told ghost stories or just listened to the music from Acong's store.

After playing two rounds of Patalunton, I decided to quit to give others a chance to play. My friend, Junior invited me to ride his bike and pedal around the town.

The national road ran alongside the river on the east side of the town proper. We started by the municipal building, which was a stone's throw from our house and facing the residence and clinic of Dr. Carlina Naldo, Municipal Health Officer, past the Catholic church, going north. The *sasalugan* or dirt road going down the river lies outside the churchyard. This place was the main thoroughfare for the folks trying to get to the other side of the river. Here, I spent a lot of time playing, for the house next to it was Mr. and Mrs. Ceferino Abordo's, who were nice enough to offer us a place to stay when I was very young. Their son, Soso became the best friend of my brother, Anton.

In this neighborhood, I spent my pre-school years with my neighbors and playmates, the Sabangan sisters, Mering and Deling. Most of our time was spent up their *sarisa* tree; gathering and eat-

In A Quiet Village

ing the red and yellow berry-like fruits. Then, there were Nelda Domingo and Charing Milan; we played with our homemade dolls in our make shift store selling weeds, guava leaves and other kinds of junk that we gathered in the neighborhood pretending that we were merchants. We also spent a lot of time in the river, which was just in our backyard. The Domingos had a tamarind tree that was known to be the sweetest in town. Of course, this tree was not spared from the kids in the neighborhood.

Past the Milan house was the store of the Guintos where we bought candies and cookies. One of the daughters, Carmencita, was also my friend. We went to church together for mass and attended the catechism lessons from Auntie Elen [Miss Mañago]. When we were older, we both became members of the Sodality of the Children of Mary.

After half a mile, the road went on a curve to the left. On the right side of the curve was a steep ravine where a tall, old *balete* tree stood menacingly. Folks say that there was a K*apre* [a big black man smoking a cigar] living in this tree and on some nights, when it was dark and raining, one could see the tip of his cigar glow, amidst the flutter of the *alitaptaps* that engulfed the *balete*. There were no houses nearby and kids were scared to pass by this place especially at night. We whirled through as fast as we could pedal, as I closed my eyes with fear, waiting for the K*apre* to grab me. We passed through safely and continued on.

The house of *Manang* Kandra soon appeared. Kandra was a regular in our household. She went to the house every morning to see if we had soiled clothes that needed laundering. She would pick them up in the morning and bring them back in the afternoon all nicely pressed. I could remember how Manang Kandra rescued me from difficult situations when I needed my dress to be pressed immediately for a special occasion in school. We treated her as part of the family.

As we cruised along, we passed by several groups of people playing the same games of *Patalunton*. We passed by the house of the Hidalgo sisters. The oldest was Auntie Meciang, [Melecia] a schoolteacher. She was very strict, and the kids feared her. The second sister was Auntie Pacing, [Pacita] a businesswoman and her daughter Nena remains as one of my best friends. Auntie Pacing's husband died while on a business trip in the province of Isabela during the Japanese occupation. She also had a son, Cesar who died from a car accident. Auntie Saning [Susana] is the youngest. She was also a teacher who grilled us in the *Balarila*, the Tagalog grammar, our national language, and in Arithmetic.

At the northern end of town was the Farmacia Sayo, the only drugstore in Aritao. I remembered this place very well for on several occasions, Inang would ask us to buy some medicines for my sick brothers in the dark of the night with only a flashlight or a lantern to light the way. This was about one and a half kilometers from our house and we have to hike to get there.

We turned around to go back and this time we took the back road, which ran alongside the mountain, known to us as Bantay Lakay. The elementary school loomed on the right side. Under the glow of the moonlight, I could see the tall grass alongside the fence. Here, we built our *nests* and ate our *baons* during recess.

The intersection with the narrow dirt road going to the *Kampo Santo* soon came to view. This was another scary place with a lot of trees, and no houses, not even the full light of the moon could brighten the darkness around. When telling ghost stories, several kids who lived in the neighborhood would tell us that they could hear crying and moaning in the middle of the night from the cemetery. Again, I closed my eyes as we passed, feeling the goose bumps all over me.

Next is the market place, which is empty at this time. Past the market is the intersection going to the barrio of Kirang. This road continues to the mountain towns of Pingkian and Kayapa and to Baguio City via the Ambuklao Dam.

We reached the end of the road and turning left would be where the Lopezes have their residence. Don Cosme, the family patriarch was the only person I knew who was addressed as "*Don*" in the whole Aritao [The other one was Don Lope Sayo of barrio Banganan] as it was known that they were the richest clan. His daughter Zening is a cousin of my friend Nelda and she would occasionally come to play with us when she came to visit. Adjacent to their house was the sari-sari store of the Navarros.

In A Quiet Village

The Mabungas' and the Javiers' were across the intersection. Miss Irene Mabunga was our teacher in Grade One. I believe all the folks in Aritao passed through her in the first grade. Her brother, Pedro, was a captain in the Philippine Army and consequently, their family have been harassed and persecuted by the Japanese during the war. Adjacent to the Javiers' were the Gomez and Bungubung houses and vulcanizing shop.

Another left-turn brought us back to our neighborhood. Adjacent to our house on the right side is the sari-sari store and bakery of Hiaba, our Chinese friend, then the residence of the Leprosos and the house and tailor shop of Mr. And Mrs. Alfonso Villafuerte, who are my parents *inaanak sa kasal*,[godchildren in marriage] thus ,we called them *kuya* and *ate*. Kuya Ponso was a tailor and I remember Tatang going to his shop whenever he needed a suit we call A*mericana. K*uya Ponso will make one specially tailored for him.

The town was rather small and it took us only about half an hour to circle it. There were a few children left playing. Some of the folks have gone home. Tata Acong's store was still open but the music has ceased. Those who were not working in the morning lingered to enjoy the rest of the night. The moon was almost setting but I wanted to stay some more to gaze at her as she continued her journey towards the western skies. Soon she would disappear behind the mountains of the Caraballo to end one beautiful, peaceful night.

Karayan
(River)

I finished my umpteenth jump from the cliff into the warm, balmy water at the deep bend of the river. As I was treading in the water, I was startled when the church bells rang the 12:00 noontime. I heard someone calling my name, "Nisaaaaa! Nisaaa!" When I looked at the top of the cliff, I saw Inang; her right hand on her waist and her left hand was waving a bamboo stick at me. I was so busy swimming and jumping off the cliff, I did not realize that it was already noon. Inang assigned me the task of cooking lunch that day. Tatang usually came home for lunch at 12:00 noon. He was supposed to bring his friend Mr. Dangilan, Postal Supervisor from the capital town of Bayombong, for lunch on this particular day that is why Inang was so angry when she did not find me at home.

    I hurried to change my wet clothes and bravely went up to accept Inang's fury in the form of a couple of whacks of the bamboo stick she was carrying. When Inang got home and did not find me, she proceeded to prepare the lunch meal. Then, knowing where to find me, she went to the river where I was swimming with the other kids.

    The lure of the river was irresistible to us. Right after a heavy rain or a storm, the river swelled and got muddy, and the current became strong and swift. Usually during a storm, a lot of banana trees got uprooted. The children would remove the leaves and drag the trunk into the river and used it as floats to ride the current. This was very dangerous and our parents were constantly reminding us to refrain from this practice but to no avail. It has been reported that one of the kids from the barrio drowned while riding the current but this did not discourage us. All we thought of was the fun and the adventure.

The river divided the town proper and the rice fields. Beyond the rice fields were the small barrios of Bagbag, Casay, Comon, Gasajas, Tucanon, Tabueng, and then the mountain range of the Caraballo. Comon was guarded by a mountain with big boulders of black stones, commonly known as Comon Rock. As children, we often held our picnics there and discovered the big boulders of rock scattered all over, thus, we named this mountain Comon Rock.

When the weather was fine, the river was calm and the water very clear. You could see the big gray and white stones as well as the smaller rocks at the bottom. There was the section of the river that went into a bend against the cliff and this was deep enough for us to dive or jump. We called this section the *lipnuk*.

The lipnuk was usually the noisiest area in the river with the screaming, yelling and laughter of everyone. The teenagers and grown ups take turn in climbing the cliff and jumping into the deep section of the water or pushing each other off the cliff.

Most of the boys were naked. Once in a while, we could see some teenage boys with a piece of string tied to their not so private part, an indication that they just had their circumcision. The little girls were either naked or have their panties on. The teenage girls wear their chemise and the young and older women use a straight piece of cloth called *bidang* to wrap around their bodies for privacy.

The shallow part of the river was almost knee deep, littered with all kinds of stones of different sizes. Here, the little kids swam, played, or just horsed around. Some of them tried their luck in catching the tiny fish called *bunog* as they hid between the stones, using their fingers or a small net called the *batbateng*. This area was also used for laundering clothes.

Doing the laundry was considered a duty and a pleasure. It was not unusual for one to spend the whole day in the river to wash the clothes. First, the big, smooth stones were put together to build a place where one can anchor the *batya*, a wide basin that holds the

In A Quiet Village

dirty clothes. The biggest and flattest stone was used to lay the soapy clothes to be beaten with a wooden paddle called *palo-palo*, to squeeze out the dirt. After the clothes were soaped, they were spread out under the sun for bleaching. This will take about a half-hour before the clothes were rinsed. This vacant time provided one the opportunity to join the others for a dip in the waters. After the clothes were bleached, these were rinsed and beaten, then again spread out to dry. It was a beautiful sight to see a rainbow of colors from the clothes drying under the sun.

The women, young and old, went to the river to wash clothes and to socialize as well. Young men (mainly suitors) dropped by. They pretend to take a swim, bathe their carabaos, or fetch water from the shallow wells whenever they knew that the young woman they were courting or their sweetheart was in the river with her wash.

With my friends, Nelda and Charing, I frequented the river to picnic and to fetch water with our clay jars *(karamba)*. We built our own wells by digging a small hole at the banks then lined these holes with tiny stones. The water that seeped through looked very clear. We would fill our jars, then will join the others in the lipnuk, jumping and swimming until we got so tired and exhausted, or until our folks came for us with their *pamalo* [bamboo sticks]. Sometimes, we brought something to eat, like the *kanin-matamis-tubig* that Tatang told us was "*gatas ng tigre*" to cajole us into eating it. Actually, this is a concoction of burned rice, sugar and water. In retrospect, this actually tasted good.

The karayan played a major role in the lives of the people. Farmers nearby use the water to irrigate their farms. The seasonal floods brought about by the monsoon rains served to fertilize the *taltalon* [rice fields] where rice and vegetables were the main products. After the rice was harvested, the farmers planted vegetables, onions, tomatoes, or other root crops. This was called crop rotation and was believed to keep the soil fertile.

During typhoons, the river really got flooded and the water became so strong that traffic to and from the town halted to a standstill. Nobody would dare cross the raging waters. For years, the authorities tried but were unable to build a bridge that could withstand the strong current.

Leonisa S. Merced-Malana

After the storm and the water has receded, the *karayan* would come alive again with the traffic of *kalesas* [horse drawn carriage], *karitons* [carabao drawn carts], *patuke's* [carabao pulled sled], and of people crossing by foot carrying their goods in baskets on top of their heads.

And that's how life went on by the river, our *Karayan*.

Fiesta

The November chill was a welcome sign that Christmas was near. However, the excitement was doubled by the anticipation of the celebration of the town and patron saint fiesta. In the 1700s the Dominican missionaries assigned Saint Catherine of Alexandria, virgin and martyr, as the patron saint of Aritao and her feast was celebrated on November 25th each year [V].

We stayed late in school practicing our part in the folk dance and calisthenics demonstration that would be presented as part of the fiesta celebration. All school children from the Central School as well as from the barrios were expected to participate and compete for these events. Our teacher, Miss Melecia Hidalgo taught us the folk dance *Tagala* as our presentation. The other students were practicing their calisthenics with dumb bells and rings made of rattan.

Earlier in the afternoon, a truck with a speaker went around town announcing a free movie at the town plaza. Since there was no electricity in town, much more a movie house, this event was most welcome. The show was offered by a drug company selling the vitamin B complex known as *Tiki Tiki Manuel Zamora*.

We hurried home and after supper, my friends and I ran to the plaza in order to get a choice spot in the grass covered ground. Soon after you could feel the exodus of the people carrying their kerosene lanterns, candles or flashlight to light their way towards the plaza.

Leonisa S. Merced-Malana

The show consisted of Mickey Mouse cartoons and an old movie starring veteran actor, Rogelio dela Rosa and his leading lady, Carmen Rosales. The show was of course preceded by and interspersed with the Tiki Tiki advertisement, a vitamin that was supposed to prevent and cure a Vitamin B deficiency called Beri-beri.

As the fiesta approached, people got busy preparing for the stages where special presentations would take place. In one corner of the plaza, the Isinays were building the stage for the *Moro Moro*, a musical presentation compared to an operetta or sarzuela depicting the lives and wars of a kingdom. The cast was composed of a king, queen their princes and princesses and their warriors. The lyrics was written in the Isinay dialect and the costumes were of bright, glittering reds, yellows, green, silver and gold complete with their combat weapons of sabers, spears and shields. The music was provided by the local band.

On another section of the plaza were two stages built for the orchestral presentation called *Swayan*. This was a dialog between two orchestras similar to a debate in that the participants answered each other as they played their musical numbers. This was supposed to be spontaneous as the singers composed their songs to respond to what was delivered by the opposite orchestra. The swayan usually lasts the whole night or as long as there were listeners or audiences. Although we would not be present in the plaza, we would be awake most of the night as the stage was just across the road from our house.

Several days before the Fiesta, streets near the church and plaza would be closed to traffic so that merchants can put up their *toldas* for their merchandise. These merchants travel from town to town to sell their wares during the fiestas. There were also booths for the *beto-beto*, a form of gambling using dice, complete with displays of stuffed animals, china and glass sets and other gadgets as prizes.

Included in the entertainers was *Kiko,* the ventriloquists' sidekick and main attraction, very popular especially with the kids. There were also magicians and herbal medicine vendors featuring demonstrations of instant cures for using their medicines.

At night, the plaza would be full where there were shows featuring gay and lesbian performers. These men were beautifully

In A Quiet Village

made up and one cannot distinguish whether they were males or females. They can sing and dance and I usually stayed up all night watching their show.

Weeks before the fiesta, the town and each barrio would elect a local beauty to compete for the crown of Miss Aritao. This was a fundraising event and each candidate raised the money thru different means like selling tickets, asking for voluntary contributions or holding a benefit dance. The benefit dance was the most popular among the fundraising events and the main attraction was the selling of boxes prepared by the candidates. The boxes, beautifully wrapped were auctioned off to the highest bidder and as people bid, the bidder will have the privilege of dancing with the owner of the box until he was outbidded by another. Sometimes, this event could get too emotional and competitive as competing suitors get entangled into rivalry.

The coronation of Miss Aritao and her princesses would occur the night before the day of the Fiesta. The much anticipated grand ball was held at the town plaza attended by the dignitaries and guests from neighboring towns including the Congressman, Governor or other important people.

Nine days before the fiesta, a novena to St. Catherine was held every evening. The solemn high mass that will be celebrated on the feast day by itself required weeks of preparation. First, there would be a daily practice of the Latin mass by the choral group. At the same time, Auntie Elen Mañago and her crew would be busy preparing and decorating the altars. The mass was usually concelebrated by visiting parish priests and sometimes with the Bishop as the main celebrant.

After the High Mass, the parade follows. The floats, led by the town officials and representatives from the different civic organizations show the artistic expressions from the local groups as they decorate their respective entries. The floats of the two princesses precede that of the queen. Bands from the different schools or organizations would take this opportunity to show off their skills.

The afternoon after the parade will be the competition for the different games such as basketball, volleyball, and softball as well as other contests for the children. Our neighbor, Apped, was not only a good softball pitcher but she also had a beautiful voice and she usually competed in both events. We would choose the best spot in the playground to cheer for her during the competitions.

Late in the 1960s a new parish priest was assigned to Aritao. Since the church could no longer accommodate the growing number of parishioners, this was demolished and a modern edifice was constructed. Concurrent with this, the Patron Saint, St. Catherine was replaced by St. Joseph, thus changing the fiesta date to March 19th, the feast of St. Joseph.

I suppose it really would not matter who our patron saint was. The townspeople celebrated our town fiestas with the same anticipation and fervor year after year.

Palengke (Market)

The early morning chill crept in the valley overnight. I shifted my body towards the left side of the bed and pulled on the covers that I shared with my brother, Anton. The cold was bone chilling as I tried to grasp more sleep. The croaking of the frogs by the riverbank kept me awake until the wee hours of the morning. Suddenly, the quiet of dawn was pierced by the cry of the boy selling *pandesal*. "*Pandesal, napudot pay*", meaning, the bread was fresh from the oven and is still hot. In a while, our dog, Kibul, started barking and was joined by the others in the neighborhood. The sun was slowly creeping up the eastern horizon.

As I became fully awake, I realized that it was Sunday morning. The native Igorots have descended in the valley bringing their handicrafts and farm products to sell in the market. The arrival of the Igorots was always heralded by the dogs' barking as they would when strangers came to town. Aritao is a small town and unlike the other more progressive towns in the province, there were only three market days during the week and the biggest one was on Sundays. On this day, merchants from the neighboring towns also came to sell their wares.

The church bells tolled, announcing the early mass at six o'clock. I can hear Inang in the kitchen preparing breakfast of *sinangag* [fried rice], *daing* [dried fish] and coffee. She usually got up early on market days for soon, Juan, the *kuchero*, will be arriving with his *kalesa*. Inang has contracted Juan to haul her merchandise to the *palengke* where she had a space to display her *paninda*. I looked forward to this day as I was expected to help out, but first I had to attend the Sunday mass before I could do anything else.

Today's *tiangge* will be good. Yesterday, Inang arrived from Manila with new bales of clothes, shoes and *chinelas*. Her chinelas, which were specially made in Baliuag, her hometown, was very popular among her customers in the valley. The bales of clothes were the newest in fashion as she got them from Lucing, a merchant from Tabora in Manila.

I loved to sit quietly in one corner of the store and watch the people milling around. There I could get first hand news as they went on with their bargaining and cajoling with a lot of *tsismis* in between. The transactions went fast. With Inang's *suki* [regular customers with good credit], they don't have to pay right away. She will just enter their names in her *listahan* and after payday, my sister Mercy and I went to their homes and collected the payments [*agsingir*].

I loved the palengke. I loved to go around and see all the fresh vegetables spread on the ground for sale. There were fresh bamboo shoots, eggplants, bitter melon, squash, young tamarind leaves, *saluyot, gabi* and other exotic vegetables, including different species of seaweeds. I loved to see the live fish, different kinds of snails such as the *bisukol, agurong, liddeg* and frogs that the folks caught overnight with the help of their lanterns.

The palengke was never dull. The fruits and vegetables sold vary according to the seasons. You will know Christmas was at hand when you smelled the *pinipig* in one of those baskets. Pinipig was made of young sweet rice harvested and burned until the grain fell off the stalk. This was then pounded until the husks came off. The smell of burned rice stalks brought a nostalgic reminder that Christmas was near.

In May, after the first rainfall, there was an abundance of *abal-abal*. This is a member of the beetle family and was considered a delicacy. Sometimes, I joined the other children in crossing the river to catch these elusive creatures. When the sun went down, the abal-abal came out in droves flying over the rice fields or cogon

In A Quiet Village

grass that grew along the banks. They linger for only a brief period of time, then would suddenly disappear under the leaves, after which, it would be very difficult to find them. You have to be quick in catching them. A special lure made of a treated bark called *kiddeng* is used to trap them. The catch is then placed on a bamboo tube called *tubong*.

Mangoes are in season during the months of March until August. In the early part of the year, when the mango trees start to bloom, they were fumigated to ensure a bountiful harvest. Mangoes were consumed either green or golden ripe, but the best ones were the *manibalang* or medium ripe. The green and medium ripe mangoes were eaten with a dip called *aramang*, or fermented tiny shrimps in salt. We bought this from *Nana* Turyang, our neighbor, who hailed from the province of Pangasinan where the best aramangs came from.

During this time of the year, there were also other fruits such as *santol, sineguelas, duhat* and *singkamas*. *Santol* has several slimy seeds as big as the thumb and the children enjoyed swallowing them to the horror of their parents. The duhat is similar to the cherry except that it was dark purple and you could tell when someone had been eating it by the purple color of his or her teeth. *Singkamas* is a root crop. The skin is easily peeled off to expose the crunchy, pearly and succulent white meat.

September to November is the time for *lanzones*. This fruit tree is very hard to grow and only thrived in the province of Laguna and other parts of Mindanao. The meat of this fruit is soft and crystal white, divided in about five segments.

Legend says that the name *lanzones* came from the word *lason* [poison]. In the town of Laguna where this tree originated, the people who ate its fruit died. One day, during a famine, a beautiful woman appeared in town. As she picked to eat the fruit, people warned her that this was poisonous. Instead of discarding it, she brushed her hand across the fruit and ate it. The people were surprised that she did not die and they started eating it too. They also noticed that the meat was divided into five segments similar to the lady's fingers. Shortly after, the woman disappeared and was never seen again. They then called the fruit lanzones[vi].

Leonisa S. Merced-Malana

Inang gave me the sign that it was time to go around and buy our foodstuff. I grabbed my basket, proceeded to the meat section and bought two kilos of pork and some neck-bones from our suki, Mrs. Angudong. Then I went to the fresh vegetable section to get fresh *rabong, saluyot,* tomatoes, *pechay* and *malunggay.* The saluyot and rabong made a good combination especially when cooked with broiled fish, either the *dalag* or *hito,* or one could also substitute smoked fish called *tinapa.* In addition, I got some tamarind blossoms to be added to the pork neck-bones that will be cooked as *sinigang,* Tatang's favorite dish of soured soup.

The *kakanin* section was always a must. My favorites were the *suman-sa-ibos,* [rice cake wrapped in palm leaves], *puto / kutsinta* [blended and steamed rice cakes] and *tupig* [sweet rice flour with shredded coconut wrapped in banana leaves and roasted in charcoal]. I came across a lady selling boiled corn on the cob and boiled peanuts. I added these to complete my basket. Nearby, I noticed a lady with her basket lined with banana leaves containing *binubudan*, prepared from cooked rice fermented until it becomes soggy and juicy. Eating this will result in a drunken like state as the fermentation makes the rice like wine. Continued fermentation will yield a strong drink called *tapey,* with higher alcohol content.

The church bells rang. It was 12:00 o'clock noon. Soon it will be time to go home. I began putting back the unsold merchandise in their boxes. The palengke was over. There will be two days of rest before the next market day on Wednesday. Juan arrived and the merchandise was loaded back in the kalesa for the short trip home. I was tired but happy as I always enjoyed going to the Palengke.

Friends and Neighbors

The people we met and knew so well made our little town of Aritao very special indeed. Small as it might be, there were different groups that comprised the population. The native Isinays were the heart of the village but steadily, the growing number of *estrangeros* from other provinces made Aritao somewhat of a melting pot. The Merceds from Zambales and Bulacan were really strangers in my hometown, as were families that we grew up with. The Dulays and Serquinias were from Pangasinan, the Hidalgos from La Union, the Guintos and Chancocos from Pampanga, the Del Rosarios and Navarros from Nueva Ecija and many families from the Ilocos region, all strangers in that teeny bit of a town. There were also some families from other countries like China and India.

Our first year in Aritao demanded a lot of adjustments for Tatang and Inang; first of all, they did not speak the vernacular language of Ilocano and the customs of the people were very different. Our first neighbors and friends helped my parents in the transition and adjustments to our new environment.

Mrs. Cornelia Dalan was one of Inang's first acquaintances and friend. She was the Puericulture Center Nurse and her husband, Eladio worked with Tatang in the Post office. Then there were Juan and Martha Apolinar, the Juan Daniels, the Ceferino Abordos, Honorato Montefalco and family. Daniel Sabangan and family, Lorenzo Lejao and family, the Uy Kays [pronounced Wee Kay],

Carlina Valera Naldo, M.D.

In A Quiet Village

Mr. and Mrs. Crispin Domingo, the parents of my friend Nelda, Mr. and Mrs. Pedro Milan, parents of Charing, and many others who played important roles in our lives. Mr. Abordo and Mr. Montefalco were elected Municipal Mayors. Mr. Lorenzo Lejao was the Municipal Secretary.

Dr. Carlina Valera came to Aritao as the first physician and was assigned as the Municipal Health Officer. She just completed her medical training when she came to stay with us. She was also single. She was the first person to own a car in town. After school and on weekends, I accompanied her in her rounds, visiting the sick. I became her assistant and she taught me how to take temperatures, pulse and blood pressure. She also taught me how to dress wounds and give injections. One of the memorable experiences I had with her was when I assisted her in performing an autopsy on a couple of farmers who were beheaded by the Ilongots. I was in high school and was scared to death but at the same time was very curios and eager to learn. She became my inspiration in pursuing a Nursing career. The best thing I enjoyed so much was riding in her black Ford as we went visiting her patients around town as well as in the barrios. She became Inang's best friend. She was the one who taught us to cook *pinakbet* the Ilocano way. Later on, she met a lawyer, Attorney Benjamin Naldo who she later married. They had three children, Ramon, Dalisay, and Aurora.

Mr. and Mrs. Fermin Austria was our neighbor and a compadre of Tatang and Inang. My brother Bing was their godson. Although we were good friends and their daughter Apped was one of my playmates, I seldom went to their house. This was because the coffin of Mrs. Austria's father was kept in their living room for reasons I never understood. He was Mr. James Thomas, an African American .The presence of the coffin in their living room gave a kind of eerie feeling for us kids.

Our neighbor, *Hiaba* was a Chinese national who came to the Philippines from Mainland China. He was soft spoken, friendly and intelligent. Every evening, after we have finished our prayers, he would come to the house and spend the rest of the evening talking with Tatang. He owned the bakery by the house that he was renting from Inang. Most of his chats with Tatang were focused on the current political situation but the conversation would always shift to his hometown in China. He also found time to play with us children, and sometimes he would act as a bouncer when my brothers really got unruly and out of control. He taught us how to count and say simple phrases in Chinese.

Boombing was the baker. From our house, we could hear the sound of dough as he picked it up and threw it on the table as part of the kneading process. Not long after, we would smell the aroma of freshly baked bread and sometimes, when you stand by Boombing's place, you might be lucky to be the first one to *tikim* [taste] the sample. Sometimes, Inang would get up early and get the fresh baked bread from Boombing, then will slip the hot bread thru our mosquito net while we sleep. This was her form of waking us up in the early morning.

Payat was the other Chinese who stayed in the lower level of our house. He was very skinny that is why people called him *payat*, [skinny]. Sometimes, out of curiosity, I would lie on my stomach on the split bamboo floors and peep down to watch him eat. I could not figure out how he was able to eat his *lugao* using a pair of chopsticks. He was a quiet person but very friendly. Unlike Hiaba, we did not know too much about him. His business was confined to buying and selling palay.

Ruperto Gatchalian, Jr. was my childhood playmate. He was called "Junior" by everybody. He was also my classmate from elementary school thru high school. Since their house was in front of ours, we spent a lot of playing hours together, whether we played *linnemmengan* [hide and seek], *patalunton*, or *holen* [marbles]. When we were old enough to walk long distance, we would go to their *bangkag* [orchard] in barrio Kirang to gather different kinds of fruit. Our favorite past time was to ride around town in his bike. His youngest brother Tabyong was the playmate of my brother Anton and my sister Mercy. Junior was one of five boys and an elder sister, Manang Caring who was the eldest in their family. She was later married to Manong Cariong, one of the sons of Don Cosme Lopez, and had to move out leaving the Gatchalian family to the five sons. Soon, Manang Osing [Josefina Epistola] came to join the family when she married Manong Peping, the eldest boy.

In A Quiet Village

I could remember every day at dawn, one of the brothers would drive their herd of carabaos to their *pasto* [pasture] in barrio Banganan on the northern part of Aritao, and like clockwork, the herd was driven back to town at dusk arriving just about the time when the church bells would ring the Angelus at 6:00 pm.

Also included in my circle of friends were Romy Montefalco, Timoteo Aleman [Timot] and Doming, Junior's younger brother. Then there were other friends like Joaquin Chancoco, Carayo Caoile, Ising and Beling Bungubung and Manang Oriang Leprozo, our neighbor.

Mr. Calixto Mequin, the mail carrier would stop by Inang's store after making his rounds delivering mail. He loved to test our skills by asking us questions and problems in Arithmetic, Geography or Current Events. Most of the time, when I was able to solve the problems first, he would give me that grin of approval, at the same time he would shake his head or grit his teeth towards the others who failed to answer correctly. Everybody knew Mr. Mequin. He was a tall, burly man with a mean look as he always scared the children by yelling at them and shooing them off. He was also unique in that, rain or shine, he was always wearing his boots as he went around delivering the letters. I figured that the boots were mainly to protect him, not only from the rain but also from the dogs who would attempt to take a bite off his legs.

I can never forget how Mr. Mequin played a significant role in my life. I was twelve years old and finally graduated from Elementary School in 1948. I was very excited because soon I would have to choose where to enroll for my High School education. Having been a product of the Central Luzon Agricultural School [CLAS] in Muñoz, Nueva Ecija, Tatang decided that I should study there.

CLAS was quite far from home; we had to travel by bus to the next province of Nueva Ecija, crossing the mountainous road of the Caraballo and Dalton Pass. The trip was about five hours. When we finally got there, Tatang arranged for me to stay with one of the faculty members as one of their boarders.

After my enrollment was arranged and tuition fees were paid, Tatang left to go back to Aritao. Soon after he left, I suddenly felt a pang of terrible loneliness and a longing for home. I cried all day and all night and could not eat. My landlord did not know what to do. In my mind, I did not want to go to school anymore. I just wanted to go home. However, this was my first time to be away and I did not know how to get public transportation. Besides, Tatang and Inang would surely be upset if I did not continue my studies as planned.

Suddenly, one morning, as I was sitting quietly on the porch, I could hardly believe my eyes as I saw Mr. Mequin approaching. I jumped and fled to embrace him. I was so happy to see a familiar face from home. I cried as I told him I wanted to go home and that I did not care to go to school anymore. Poor Mr. Mequin became very uneasy and did not know what to do with this unexpected situation. He was also concerned that Tatang would not approve of my going home as he was sent there just to visit me. However, I was very determined and my landlord finally agreed that I should go.

I quickly packed my belongings and with Mr. Mequin, we proceeded to the waiting station of the Rural Transit for the next trip home. As soon as we left the CLAS compound, for the first time in two weeks, I felt a huge sigh of relief. I did not care what punishment Tatang and Inang would give me. I just wanted to go home.

I was very quiet as the bus tackled the dusty road of the Caraballo, with a lot of apprehension, not knowing how Tatang and Inang might react to my coming home. I tried to rehearse in my mind what to say. In a way, I felt very guilty for failing my parents' wishes. On the other hand, I would not have been able to concentrate on my studies because of this terrible feeling of homesickness.

When we arrived and I finally got off the bus, I approached the house quietly. Inang and Tatang were at home and they were surprised to see me. Mr. Mequin tried to explain to them the circumstances as best as he could. I was waiting for the scolding from both of them but this did not happen as they fully understood my feelings, or maybe, they also missed me when I was away as much as I missed them.

Never did I realize how closely knit we were as a family until I left for CLAS. I was also very thankful that Inang and Tatang took the incident in stride and made other plans for me to continue my studies.

Author at 14 years old

Farewell To Childhood

I enrolled at St. Mary's High School in the capital town of Bayombong, about thirty kilometers from home and short of an hour's travel by jeep. I stayed with the Franciscan nuns in the convent. This was an entirely new routine for me but I did better because I was able to go home on the weekends.

Every morning at about 5:30 am, the nun in charge of the boarders would knock on the door to wake us up. We would jump out of bed and do our morning routine of getting ready for the day such as washing our face, brushing our teeth and putting on our High School uniform of maroon and white. Then she would ring a small bell and we would go down the stairs and queue for the chapel for the morning mass. After the mass, we would file down the aisle to go to the dining room for our breakfast, then after a short prayer, the nun will escort us to the High School compound for our classes.

The evening routine will be similar. The Angelus was always prayed, then the little bell will announce supper time followed by study time and bedtime. I could say that we lived by the bell but it did not take long for me to adjust to this kind of routine.

I studied at St. Mary's for a year but the following school year, I transferred to the Nueva Vizcaya Institute in Aritao. This High School has just opened a few years and was still in its stage of development. Since I don't have to leave home, I was very happy and excited in anticipation of the opening of school.

Leonisa S. Merced-Malana

Finally, I met my new teachers; Miss Apolinaria Pimentel [History], Mr. Benjamin Ibasco [General Science], Mr. Claro Mendoza [Geometry], Mr. Servillano Pablo [National Language], Mr. Juan Mabunga [Literature], Mr. Antonio Serquinia [Algebra] and Mr. Basilio Poyatos [Economics]. Our principal was Mr. Anastacio Soriano.

Since I did not start High School at NVI, I was considered as one of the new students together with others who came from different parts of the country. They were Minandang Alonto, from Mindanao, Jose Cardona, from Manila and Antero delos Reyes, Jr. from Lopez, Quezon. There were also students from the neighboring barrios that I have to meet for the first time or old acquaintances that would become my classmates. To mention a few, there were Josefina Nidua, Pedro de Leon, Mauro Obaña, Edgar Poyatos, and our special classmate, Mr. Fructuoso Carreon, a very respectable, elderly gentleman from barrio Cutar. Because of his age, he became a father figure to us and I don't know how he was able to put up with a bunch of teenagers for classmates. He taught us some Philippine folkdances when we had to perform on special occasions such as town fiestas, Juniors' prom and Foundation Day.

Teresita Epistola was one of my classmates who became my closest friend. Every school day, she dropped by the house on her way to school and waited for me so we could walk together. Before class starts, we would sit on the grass-covered ground in the schoolyard to study our lessons or chat with our other classmates while waiting for the bell.

One morning, Tessie and I were assigned to sing a duet during the flag raising ceremony. We started to sing, "when the day is nearly over" from the song "A Child's Fancy," but we never made it past the second stanza. For some reason, one of us started to laugh and we ended up giggling and as much as we tried to continue with the song, we could not do it. We ended up going back to our line formation and the flag raising ceremony went on without our song.

The years I spent at NVI were full of joy, anticipation, new friends and new experiences as I met the challenges of my adolescent years. First were the physical changes that were slowly becom-

In A Quiet Village

ing noticeable including the annoying and embarrassing pimples that suddenly pock marked my face. Then I noticed that Inang was becoming more picky and careful with the friends I went with, to the point that sometimes she would even ask our Principal, Mr. Soriano, to keep an eye on me.

One evening, during a fundraising ball for one of the candidates for the fiesta queen, some of my friends decided we should go and watch. I was perched comfortably on a windowpane of our school where the benefit ball was being held when a friend approached me and invited me to dance. I called him Efan, short for Juan Gabuat. I was appalled at the idea, I thought he was joking but I noticed he was serious. I got nervous as Tatang might be around and that Inang will surely be furious once she learned of this. I was not even dressed properly as we were just there to gawk and watch. I looked around and when I was sure Tatang was not there, I came down the window and danced a few steps to the tune of Tennessee Waltz. That was my first dance and I was barely fourteen.

The one thing that bothered me a lot was the observation that Inang and I seemed to disagree more often with the friends I went with. I felt that someone I liked would not always be acceptable to her and the ones she liked were not exactly the ones I would like to be with. In retrospect, I suppose that for any mother's heart, no one would be ever "good enough" for her first daughter.

Gone were the days when I was free to run around and play with my friends, or go to the river and spend the whole morning in the lipnuk or climb the fruit trees in our neighbor's backyard or stay up on moonlit nights without being watched. Yes, I missed all those freedoms but I guess I had to let go and face the future. Life goes on and does not wait for anyone. The world waits for no one, but I cannot help but take one last nostalgic look at innocence.

Reference

[i] Inscriptions from the monument at Balete Pass

[ii] Philippines hand-book Carl Parkas, Moon publication INC. P-278

[iii] History of Aritao by Emilio Telentio, Gergorio F. Zaide, 1953

[iv] Philippines hand-book Carl Parkas, Moon publication INC. P-278

[v] IBID

[vi] The lives of the saints by Omer Englebert, David McKay Company, INC- fifth edition 1955

[vii] Mga Alamat ng Pilipino by Mario Odulio DeGusman, National book store, Manila Philippines 1972, page-27

Glossary

Abal-abal	Local edible beetles
Aglipay	A religion founded by Gregorio Aglipay
Agsingir	Ilocano term for "collect debts"
Agurong	Local fresh water shellfish with spiral shell
Al'-o	Pestle made of wood, four to five feet long
Alitaptaps	Fireflies
Alsong	Large mortar made of wood
Ama	Term of respect used before a name; literally "father"
Apog	Powder made from burned shells
Aramang	Fermented shrimp paste
Ari	King, ruler
Atang	Offering to the spirits
Ate	Elder sister
Bagoong	Fermented fish sauce
Bakya	Wooden shoes
Balarila	Grammar for the Filipino national language (Tagalog)
Balete	Banyan tree
Bandolero	Town crier
Banka	Boat
Bannawag	A variety periodical or magazine in the Ilocano dialect

Bantay	Ilocano term for mountain
Baon	Lunch box or lunch money
Batbateng	Ilocano term for fishing net
Batya	Tagalog term for a large washing basin
Beto-beto	Gambling game using dice
Bidang	Ilocano term for a simple bathing wrap
Biga-o	A circular winnowing device made with bamboo
Binubudan	Fermented rice
Bisukol	Ilocano term for fresh water snail
Bunog	Small fresh water fish
Bunton	Ilocano term for termite mound
Caballero	Fire tree distinguished for its red, fiery blossoms
Daing	Dried fish
Dalag	Mudfish
Darak	Rice bran
Dinggen yu kailian	Hear ye, townspeople!
Duhat	Fruit compared to a berry, usually purple
Duyan	hammock
Estrangeros	Strangers
Ga'bi	Root crop similar to sweet potato
Galem	Preparing land using cow manure
Ga-wed	Leaf as an ingredient of mama'
Ginatan	Sweet rice cooked in coconut milk
Gugo	Shampoo from the bark of a tree
Guisantes	Peas
Herbolario	Herbalist, one who cures using local herbs
Hilot	Untrained healer using massage technics
Hito	Fresh water catfish
Holen	Marbles
Iglesia Ni Cristo	Religion founded by Felix Manalo
Igorots	Natives of the Cordillera mountain range
Ilocanos	Filipinos from the Ilocos region
Ina	Mother
Inaanak sa kasal	Godchild through one's marriage
Inang	Mother

Isinay	Local ethnic tribe of Aritao
Kababata	Childhood friend
Kaibaan	Evil spirits
Kaimito	Local fruit
Kakanin	Rice cakes
Kalabasa	Squash
Kalesa	Ornate two-wheeled horse drawn carriage
Kalunay	Wild spinach
Kamote	Sweet potato
Kampo Santo	Cemetery
Kangkong	Edible vine that grows in swamps or ponds
Kanin-matamis-tubig	Rice-sugar-water
Kapote	Rain coat
Kapre	A mythical entity like a tall ogre with a horse for a head
Karamba	Earthen water jar
Karayan	River
Kariton	Carabao drawn, two-wheeled wagon
Kayu-kayu	A native call to the spirits
Kiddeng	Treated bark used to lure the edible beetles
Kuchero	Coachman usually for a horse drawn cart, kalesa
Kundiman	Classic Tagalog love songs which is sad and melancholy
Kur-it	To dig using a knife or a pointed object
Kutsinta	Steamed cake made with rice flour and lye
Kuya	Elder brother
Lakay	Old man
Lanzones	Local fruit
Lason	Poison
Liddeg	Small fresh water snail
Linnemmengan	Ilocano term for the children's game of "hide and seek"
Lipnuk	A deep
Listahan	List of a business' debtors
Liwayway	A variety periodical or magazine in the Tagalog dialect

Lola	Grandmother
Lolo	Grandfather
Lugao	Porridge
Ma-am-amlingan	Ilocano term for acquiring a disease thru a spell
Makapili	Filipino traitors or spies during the Japanese regime
Malunggay	A leafy vegetable
Ma-ma'	Beetle nut
Manang	Older sister
Manggagamud	Local witch, one who casts evil spells
Manibalang	Almost ripe
Mano	Gesture of respect to hold and touch an offered hand to one's forehead.
Merienda	Afternoon snack
Mochi	Sweet rice flour
Monay	Sweet bread
Moro-moro	A musical play presented by the Isinays during the fiesta.
Napudot pay	Ilocano term for "Still hot"
Nepnep	Continuous rain or drizzle that usually lasts for days
Ngalog	Local vine-like vegetation used for feed
Ninang	Godmother
Palengke	Market
Palo-palo	Wooden paddle commonly used to beat dirt from clothes during washing
Pamalo	A stick or bamboo used for striking someone
Pandesal	Local bread baked daily for breakfast
Paninda	Merchandise
Pasaheros	Passengers
Pataluntun	Children's game played on grids, usually at night
Patariktik	Part of the game patalunton
Patuke	Local sled
Payat	Skinny
Pechay	Chinese cabbage

Pilay	Lame; Unable to move extremities
Pinakbet	Ilocano vegetable dish
Pinipig	Local delicacy made from burned sweet rice
Pinukpok	Cloth from the fibers of the abaca plant
Purga	Laxative
Puto	Steamed rice cake
Rabong	Bamboo shoot
Sabadistas	Seventh Day Adventists
Sabungan	Cockfight arena
Saksi Ni Jeovah	Jehovah's Witness
Saluyot	Leafy vegetable that is slimy
Santol	Local fruit with thumblike seeds
Sarisa	Cherry like fruit tree
Sari-sari	Different kinds or a combination of things
Sasalugan	Slanted dirt road
Sinangag	Fried rice
Sineguelas	Local plums
Singkamas	Jicama
Sipsip	Gnat-like insect
Stampitas	Holy pictures, usually of Jesus, Mary and the saints
Suha	Grapefruit
Suki	Regular customer with good credit standing
Suman	Sweet rice cakes wrapped in banana leaves
Suman-sa-ibos	Sweet rice cakes wrapped in young coconut leaves
Suyod	Fine comb
Swayan	Ilocano literary form of sung debate
Tagalog	Main dialect chosen as core for the national language of the Philippines
Taltalon	Rice field
Tapey	Strong alcoholic concoction, fermented
Tata	Uncle
Tatang	Father
Tau	Isinay term for "our"
Tia	Aunt
Tiangge	Market

Tikim	Taste
Tinapa	Smoked fish
Tio	Uncle
Tolda	Canvas used for shelter
Tsinelas	Slippers
Tsismis	Gossip
Tubong	Hallow bamboo tube
Tupig	Sweet rice cake with grated coconut cooked by roasting
Tutubi	Dragon Fly
Upo	Gourd
Viajeros	Travelers